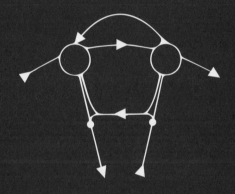

PERMANENT VOLTA

PERMANENT VOLTA
ROSIE STOCKTON

NIGHTBOAT BOOKS   NEW YORK

ISBN: 978-1-64362-075-6

Cover illustration by Mountain Pollen
Frontispiece drawing by Rissa Hochberger,
inspired by Jacques Lacan's graph of desire.

Design and typesetting by Rissa Hochberger
Typeset in Bembo and Plakette

Cataloging-in-publication data is available
from the Library of Congress

Nightboat Books
New York
www.nightboat.org

CONTENTS

HAIGIOGRAPHY

ENCRYPTION

Here we are cathected to the idea of ocean, while plums grow in a field, taking on spotted features of the night sky. Hands pick them in a language Virgil doesn't yet speak.

Imagine, the tip of a mop against skin. How the pavement skims toes. The other side of horizon. Listen, how bridges forgo the flows along their sizzling concrete. Suspended, through and through.

Asking, what can be thrown like a clog into a machine, once the machine learns to swallow the clog, energized. Updated strategies: a spilt glass of wine on the logic board. Spreading and spreading. From a crevice of a body. A moon rages, representing nothing.

Entering a windowless room, an unwitnessed wall. Taking up a pen together, the spiderweb extends from the spider, an architect that dreams. Huddling to imagine our labor before we erect it. Asked to perform a pesky witnessing, the blood unfurls. & there is always something coming. A far off siren. A bath left running will overflow.

Instead, like plums, we must prepare to resist speaking. Or anything that might be understood as spoken. Quietly addressing tongue and teeth, the taste of awakeness spreads before the horizon like seawater.

NO WAGES / NO MUSES

PROEM

un mused ethnography
of suns & smashed windows

O dead decorous & phenomenological
our wages

error cum laude
thru fog & fences

riotous our flood
sing with me—

GENRE RIOT

let's get this multitude going
w/ coffee and snacks
and this metaphysical need

I know that things can get bigger,
big enough to clash
this discord, it will be endless
buckling like water
sounding soft the din
of our titantic breathing

these conditions are threatening,
we must bring a sheath,
a rose petal tinderbox,
let our handles blur
let the latent slogan roll
become complicit with water

let's tend our bricks together,
destroy our vowels
and desire to pay our debts
sync the molecular sounds of our exhale
liquidate our cash to its pre-egoic state
set up shop in this dried up pen factory
make this shore resplendent

let's press down hard,
what we write once shows up three times
carbon paper skin, signing away our water
our bodies clash against cloth
and this is proof of being
clouds fallen around us,
sky cast off by hope

O *narrative* is printed on my breathing
O that I can't prove even this fact of sky?
we know it feelingly, glossy,
obscured light, with veils on veils,
bathing in the pavement,
hair hinged to the porch that birthed it

this is our strategic grievance,
the retaliation of the streets
a chamomile chamber with daybreak
that wreaks of nubile birds

but parallel our songs,
parallel & breathing

let's dream up what comes next—
rambunctious dust, an orchestral clash,

& they will know us
flooded with presence
hiding behind the flora we planted
thorny morning, ivy over our eyelids
let them look at us
let them ask us for our one word

O I RSVP to that bobbing chest we built
with the state's nails and history's forests
let's make room for the microphonic waves
to swallow finches, burrowed
into time's expansion
to show us our bodies
all those years from now

it is time
can't you hear that far off sound?

TACTICAL INVOCATION
in two parts

I.

LET THERE BE/COMING

let's kill our authors
I love you centuries away won't you let me
I'll be your cathartic underdog
you with your raunchier than thou attitude

O come to my island
O island, let us seduce each other

let the flowers breathe and take
let's become surge and virus
let's trip the main and shut it down

O lucky the pavement etched by your weight
I glow for you and to think I always have

where I'm marking your box on all my applications
I am citizen of your fiction
& that's where I will live

with your static layered on my static
we emit mineral and singing
make a tapestry of our static
we will emit our glory
& punishment

all definition
— no name

II.

O!

O how
I love you you angelic slut
together imagine how weighty our collective & bombed organs

what moons were our youth together?
are we animal enough to be witnessed?
like me, my fantasy body
embroidered & elliptically dug into dirt's castration

born perforated and they punish our rips
this is my tantrum. be quiet with me
and descriptive

this discipline is the least precise thing I know—
no mistaken sun to testify
no rights to sign away

but a gazillion times
I stand for you. I would & I do—
and I would too

EUNUCH OF INDUSTRY

I've got some human requirements
hornet, injury, toothbrush.

technology
invented my need and I do

I need against schedules
lodging my hunger

for you
and cement sound.

what if we kissed
in the Amazon locker?

crude oil massage, your hand lotion
on my choke points

your most fresh sacrifice
boxed like Blue Apron

there's no time to eat
rotting in a stoop's sunlight.

box trucks and networks
can be so lonesome, so owned.

& I am alone tonight,
trying to remember that

we don't want
what we think we want.

O Plato my Plato
I'm calling off our sessions

I'm blocking your image
& of all your shadows

what about the shadow
their chains cast?

HUSH LITTLE BABY /
DON'T SAY A WORD

in hung thrownness
a brick's paradise
a window's anticipation
caressed & gleeful
on the factory belt

blushing, bought, fantastical
this litany on strike
a refusal of objects glitched out
possessed & silent
in hypnotic chant

with dull rings and songless birds
with overturned carts and bulls
with a broken looking glass

humming with
the sweetest baby
in town—

    O mother
    there is a violence
    in naming
    in showing up
    to say
    can we love with inadequate politics?
    apart and pained?

    poem riveted to poem
    emerging in me this feeling
    we must invent what we see

IN/VOCATION

on my way to the grocery store
mere and betablocked

paucity erupted in me
I call on you

in the parking structure
door slammed on

thoughtful and delayed
a stranger's infrastructure

the wheel wobbling on my cart
voluptuous and prolific

to think you were in me
in my systems

I look upon the avocados
their distance

and oranges
reminding me

that we did not come
you a scarlet laureate

from similar places
a switch like me

invoke me sweet as sky
like you

and I come
I fear the future

like me
like the samples

I like your nearness
at the back of the store

you're a poor imitation
sesame chicken

alongside parody of machine
frozen fried rice

it is hollowed out
my voice distorts

like steam
with the trace I carry

of what separates
parodic this recognition

us
the literature writes

with your O
look at me

stamp my hot wax
with ruptured eyeballs

13

in turn   mangle my gaze
for this   is no way
to witness   a poem

MATERIAL MEMORY

I.

fearing a gaze that cast stone / moments of indecision
/ unable to conceive of how to forgive

      nobody could
and neither could I   decouple
      the terracotta from its dirt
      collectivize a desire so outwardly
walk the dog into abstract formalism
into a form that doesn't react   unthinkingly
      that sees itself as a subject
          sees itself as   seeing
the breakdown had layers
      I'm not sure what I said last
          night after three whiskeys
 but I knew I wanted you to find me   my
      porous body separate   and not
          there, old   ancient even.   basing identity on want
I with my sheer   impatient hopes   ripening at dawn
      how the fruit appears in   sheets of a dream
          demanding the angle demanding
the off screen gaze   castrating my self
      as audience   as dog   fixated
          on where my river stops and yours starts
I had feared my own   contagion
      until we caught it or not. expressing no symptoms, we are unable
      to know the disease.

II.

dreams emit from bodily memory / I let a gaze spread across my chest
   / a lonely window

like fashion I want to speak
        a different language and feel
                so far from it.
bask and bake in it, burn with it, be the bars
        of it, cinch it tight around a waist and
                be relieved of it. see how it makes me
see you. we freezeframe frameworks and try
        to meet in the middle. somewhere
        along the highway   the pastoral
went on strike   and like it, I mimic the fist
        assimilate the metaphor that could bridge   a gap
                memorize the shortcut in our symbolic order
        that crescendos me to clarity   with sans serif debt
        days get longer   here I stand though   somewhere
                along the edge of the city
                and even though we decided long ago
        suddenly it's hard to explain   where the kill switch is

III.

many states of water and blame / something didn't sound right
   / tones slip because the air is cold

can't forgive the walls where
         manic-effacement suffixed with
                  self and objects become un
trustworthy for what they have seen
         and done and how you have seen
                  them and how they have seen you
and when the object becomes subject thru a fucked process
         you zoom in as far as the app allows until
                  better vision comes   like how I abolished
my identity but   it keeps coming back
         with blurred color intonations and tidal
         pull where the lake is not the lake and water floats on
                  water in its most apogeic form. that's where I'd like to live—
in a palm full of ice. put a down payment on a winter current and cash
         my shit into the shore.   I press my body against the cold river rail.
                  over many years it will remind me
         what I have done when I didn't believe to be doing anything
         and like we have said to each stranger and their wallet for years—
                  do not touch me, especially
                           not with your eyes.

IV.

trade this shade of cloud for one up the road / race a feeling to the finish line

like the geese ghosted
        winter I feel external
                to the world as I pay my daily
stare into my divisive hand-held body
        of water. I want to be gone again
                st vision, never calling back this iceberg sense of border
it's so slow moving—my understanding of you and my
        self   the V shape going down south
                on me where leaves still tuck in the street and I make my bed
erratically in the mornings whether or not you are still
        in it   in the dark   how fast I imagine our pauses   gallop   and resist
                we couldn't decide on a safe   word so we didn't
stop   I've noticed sometimes when you are in it you also are not &
        we pose our mise en abyme as hypothetical to calculate risk which en
        genders risk entirely   fucking a bad mood, a misgendered memory.
I wonder   how much wind makes it through our skin and nudges our bones
        without asking   without realizing that it passes through a body at all.
at times it will push a strand of hair in one direction and another
        to make its way forward. at times it will reroute.
                I think of you   as both wind & wind
ow and I feel horizonal in relation   sheltered & swept
        always only estimating what
                feels new.

V.

warmer weather and time expansion / a river that doubles as a border
    / to experience a not-seeing

it is possible all *deja vu* is intergenerational
            we had learned it once but have forgotten
                        & we can't explain it when it's there.
mouthing the ghosts of phrases gives us the approximation of the thing
            as if there were a *thing* to approximate
you're all *olive*
            juice & I say
                ily2.
jamais vu is a phrase to designate something you think you should know
            but have the sense, when you see it,
                    that you don't.
I look out at a mist, and each day it becomes newer
            symbolic order flocks above, reflecting clamor in waves,
                    in your eyes, and in my own, my hair whips my face, my fatigue.
here are verbs that leave a residue of trauma
            I think I'll pass that along with the inheritance, which reminds me—
                    they say how pleasant the neighborhood used to be
how accumulated each brick & uninhabitable.
            aren't you worried asks a furrowed brow
                        etched from daddy landlord lifestyle elision despite
                            wages of wrinkle cream & capital.
we often are not asking the questions we mean to ask & as I stare into my mist
            I sublimate my mantra my dog takes a piss and I try to reroute habit
more accurately.
                    I miss you the most the moment before we
part   all desire mimics that brink
            before I have time to enact ritual where I mirror stage my way into language
                    & paranoid fragments, burn the toast and all the used to be's
                            that forget more than they remember

19

RE/VOCATION
for Cindy

visceral	my zenith my addled
neurology	my diet jazz
missing	heat and
a vulgar cop	in my flower bed
tonight I scroll	the block's moan and
the ice back there	ugly and divot
in the February	night sun
with a gut	pulse I drink the form
of your abrupt	nadir
how sleep	less
my plaster and	shattered glass
caving at first	glance of weedy
perennial echo	hollowing
the worker	to gain
collaborating	w insurance
on the damp	parcel
I conceive	for you
we are wrung out	on cognition
hung up on	by winter's
muted budget	cuts
the wrongest	things
made vicious	efficient

are my outfits
on the internet

dismissal
my piping

threaded
meeting

tears
leavened against

bleeding
it is clerical

nihilist
the neoliberal

administrates
song

emergency
microwave

cement enclosures
our skies

in time
how you have left

DEBT COMPLEX

m: unnatural witch
i summoned you and what

    w:

m: you are I, my hunger
pure dream, you exist & with mystique
and pen, you always already are – mine

    w: do you care more about sodomy as noun
    or verb?

m: name what you want
if i have to i will plagiarize
to make u citizen
i will

    w: *writhes, ecstatically*

m: we hear nothing
petty hysteria
what do you make of my suffering?

    w: *laughs, silently*

m: i'm willing to make a contract
i will rip open the honey for you
your mask is my stain, you are my pores
let's make a deal
baby

    w: why do we never use the whip i bought you for your birthday
    there it sits, wilting on the nail above the bed.
    you are always too tired, fuck you.

m: i thought we decided to only use it in public
from now on
your idea.
take this knife.

    w: *slicing onions, beginning to cry*

m: silent, as always
aren't we fighting
for the same thing?

    w: i fight, i hallucinate.
    the more i read, i haven't read.
    this tragedy won't write itself
    you gaslight your own narrative
    it's maddening. i don't care
    how we are read,
    only how we are reading

m: you are not perceptible
there are rooms you can't enter
your voice rings at pitches, many ears don't hear

    w: do you have anything to say? you keep changing teams.

m: you can't perform an object into object
we are matter

    w: if all people are citizens,
    is anyone really citizen?
    you need me,
    you see
    to see yourself

m: i think sodomy only exists as verb
i want to be a billionaire
i need expensive teapots, i need to skip the meetings

23

i need my reflection to move across shop windows
pure commodity

    w: i am scared, something about my soul

a glass falls from the table and shatters

m: it culminates in us all
but in none of us particularly
that is what pains me
that pain is what i cannot see

BAD SUB

m: i fear my questions reduce you.
i'd like to extend an invitation to you
to my fantasy

    w: despite the snow i come
    forbidden
    archaic, to rsvp

m: there is too much information
to celebrate anything

    w: there is love between us
    infinite
    there is after all

m: do you think
my poetry is too hostile?

    w: O honey of my masculinity
    i'll never say no.
    No,
    i am blind
    with submission
    i sit at your knees
    your fantasy of our relation determines us

m: despite the snow you came
despite the genre
now tell me – what is your real name?

    w: you are seeming out of touch
    consent is a literal myth
    yes can also mean no

m: i beg you to so you will

    w: draw me a bath and make me dinner
    i'm ready to believe, you think you hear me say,
    i'm ready to believe
    to be liberated
    each morning i wake up and pray
    organize me
    who will organize me today

m: you mock me
i like the word halt
because it is immediate
and definitive
but it feels impermanent
stop
on the other hand
may take a while
but lasts

    w: pls do both
    this is bad phenomenology
    or is it
    you are rhetorically
    ineffective?

m: you are too bratty of a bottom
you are lucky to be in my story
are you asking to get slapped?

    w: the hardest part
    for us both
    is that you need my refusal
    as much as you need me to appear

m: our dialectic it
brings me pain

w: you fall asleep first
oblique, spread too thin
the pain isn't serving you

m: unrepresentable pain
i cave in the doorway
moss grows over my eyelids
i grow later and later
it has occurred to me
in such a way i cannot commit

    w: like dirt, i think
    you need reimagining

HAIGIOGRAPHY

BAD ATTACHMENT

before the week starts   time asks of us
          when overhearing another's
interiority like it can witness   a due date only threatened
          never upheld by the soft spot I find to curl up in w/ my bad attachment
to our mutual commute   to questions like   are you where the wildfires are?
                    sinking deep into pores
I get used   to a cognitive process   how it incites our shared paranoia
                    I am one who knows
there is nothing to escape   except my own relationship   to belief
          in knowing
and when the city runs out of masks they say   don't breathe
          so deeply   which helps some
                                        like the volta helps
                    narrative articulate faulty justice
while they keep trying   to lock up the smoke   but it keeps getting out
          so we produce ourselves as   witness
to the scramble   and the weight   of the genres that fail us

31

NO MEANS

time wraps itself back up
        before the week starts so slowly it can't theorize sensation
     it can't   stay put deep in a ditch the way   I am
     backward dreaming
lunch break   my worst genre is sex   talk
     how it can't keep pace w/ the leaves' rate of bloom inert
      under my heliological need   pointing out the trancelike
underdeveloped trauma hypothesis   it is always just a hint
the way my meat doesn't want   to rearrange the words all the time
      it doesn't want lips to sip opening w/ a jaw clicking
discarded   remember how I make flowers cry on the side of
     paved parts of day   most private the time it already promised
no means no time to say when   I decide to give it all away
    and for what   I wonder   what performance
          solves the proof of interiority

HOW TO SAY YES

overhearing another's photograph   dragging public proof
it can't claim any of us *decided* this shade of red desk where the radio
        delivers narrative baby   my broken volta aches out a turn
but I'm late and dusty where I live   my boss dissolves panoptic   & the dr.'s
        note is an obsolete genre like the hospital's parking fees
where requisite lines take longer than death takes
        and the buildings blend & block
the amount of sun in the asphalt's space that slows   the flow of traffic.

when I was born they dimmed my mother's pain too far
        and there I was   claustrophobic birth canal wet tissue
on soft skull   & my mother said never
                    mind   this certification nevermind this oceanic break
like trying to unknow the big dipper   an impacted decision leaving me
a common procedure   w/ twisted chronology   coerced consent
        & a sludgy aporia as if it wasn't too late   when anyone said
                                                yes   or never

MORE MONEY

deadlines crush slowly
      like an architect's model   the beams don't come that long here
          he said   forgetting unbuilt lightning   how it shakes
my desk   failing my poem   as it tries to pass as plot and city sounds
      where I break   asleep   knowing when he is not
        watching   he is listening   to me and my
exhaustion dreams   I've adblocked them
      a costly service & my time will pay   for it
the joke of clocking in   leaves this vestibule poem broke
in the VIP room asking the boss of myself for more hours when I meant to say
                  more money
      now all I've got are   more hours when I meant more money
and just like the live record skips   my velvet genre breaks
            plot and a poem clocks in for the envoi
      that hasn't a thing to deliver   but more time
to mean
      money

WE GENRE

hard wind & this morning I archive my fossiled complaints
      expecting you to know how exactly to respond or dance
or demand   my genre   stuck in the mud of living it up
      like a bike locked to itself not going anywhere without
this desktop postit blinking my password hint
      the key's behind the sunset hanging on the bare stud
but I forget   both password and hint and am not going anywhere
      wind locked in our joints   full of this clued out   affair
like the sounds of our   pilgrimage   when I unlock one arrival narrative for us both
      and you don't know   how to respond   you must dance or genre
or start the fire to   slither & tantalize   like next year's vacation
      warm   when we can revisit
                       what the workweek prohibits

I WORK

sky crumples on the way to the workday   my least dear fact
        that only exits in its performance of my dutiful
choral citizenship proclaiming   *I work*

                                    accumulating
lush owedness   high drama in the rain   something rugged
makes   fatty my emotion   & it will only be a matter of time, they sing
        until my invocation becomes a hiring notice   and I realize
I didn't mean to ask for money   I meant to ask for a different
                                                set of relations
and if they kill me or my house   the proof of occupancy
won't be made of matter   it will be made of anger
            and mattering
is swept behind a workforce   stumbling on gritty rules and sorrow
                but   *I work*
I will have to remind them   as if to prove aliveness
                            to outshine my debt's reputation
        before the sentence begins

BEFORE THE SENTENCE BEGINS

feeling real and relevant
                    sleeves rolled high
      I name myself event   and you swallow me in
a just over there feeling   the cloud sound makes
       thrilling to wake up in your marshland rust to
                                drink your beer and soot
every note marine cast light in a happy smoldering home
      where news scrolls through our hands like water   how horror holds us on
         handheld's & with each caesura we stop   and deflect
all sloppy stumbling angelus novus ducking from blustery
                                    survival
& my curse is how I gag on my every demand   I spit up ghosts
                to make my genre perceptible
remember
           the unheard sun   finite as it is complicit
             in the naming of the event

HAVE TO HAVE

there are things I have   to have
the purple hyacinth   the false confession
     absolution   collusion   hemlock
together we cost the rain its puddled nap   dispersed into
big time hazelnut narrative   locked into botany's time
     where you get what you are   told you deserve.
I love being helpful to you   I'll clean up my hyssop
and hand it to you   a skylight for understanding   a run on sentence cut
     short & it lost some flow in my confessing this heliotrope but
there was a thing I had to have   your curfew on my radial pulse
and just one week awake to take myself out
     to sleep on salt   to find a way to wake the time
     to look upon all my flowers that refuse to identify
all   flaunting a weapon   pollen thick as song in total
arbitration   burnt like my   helenium

CYTOKINESIS

life begins in declaration, durational
      breath gaily proliferates
      the weather inside my haiku
  our seed's kink   is mitosis
      wet and procreating itself alone with its sisters
the spitting image of dreamlike   pain   & when it rains it roars it paints
me wet   it edges my comfort   in that pause of the shut door
     that restless squeeze   my partial object the shyness of my
nothing   my throaty feelings
that I couldn't   language in time like I began   before sound
you heard &   I couldn't   explain that viscous ontology
     that my being violently precedes my declarations
& in waiting it out   my stakes performed me
in bed all political damp &
       virile this scarcity   your refusal of my frame

A LIBIDINAL NOBODY

I thought you'd come for me, for me in the bar. Your light I thought would
come for me, would inhabit my hungry nobody, where we'd be object together,
we'd rot under the leaves, compost and subjectivity.

In the leaves I thought you'd come with money and gender, you'd pull over deep
inside my light. Hungry as I am, you would rot with me, we'd make money.
There we would be all nobody and together, object and object.

In the bar I was hungry for your rot, your leaves and objects, your moneyed
gender. I thought you could be inside of me, deep in my inhabit. But the
hungry rot disrupts, it disrupts the objects of our nobody.

At the bar I thought you'd leave me, gender alone. I'd compost my hungry
subjectivity, empty as a nobody, all alone, thought and money. The thought it
rots inside of me, deep in my nobody it rots like gender. The light is hunger and
object, it can't have thought to leave.

But light left me to rot there, there at the bar, with no gender and no money,
the bar where I thought you'd come, all object and hungry nobody.

EXCESS

Your sestina exceeds the bar and I sip. Windy with adjectives, my view of
thunder. In that notebook, what are you writing in that notebook. In the
notebook, that book with notes, which order are the words, which words
slight the order.

You need a word for waltz, and I said breeze, breeze or slide, march or breeze or
slide.

I sip your excess, your sestina in my notebook, the breeze it says be careful, be
careful with the sestina, the sestina in your notebook.

Where I wonder and I sip, where you got that sestina, what machine gave you
that poem. You can write a sestina, I demand, you can really write a sestina. In
your notebook with thunder, I sip windily. I waltz to think of your order, the
words in the notebook, my careful sestina.

Your breeze is marching excess, it is slow and pauseful. Always with the pauses,
you are thunder in my bar, and I sip, all excess. All excess and pause. And pause
and pause. Be careful says the sestina, marching along, with all that excess in
your notebook, with that machine that waltzes on.

No pause for the machine, only windy prediction, be careful of that word, of
that order. Excessive sestina, bent over the bar. It is writing, writing thunder and
care. I sip excess, I sip carefully, my excess. Windy with order, my excess.

HERETIC

Waking from your high pitched yawn, blinds cut up sun on your unfurled face and I feel. There is no looking at sleeping, there is no tracing your elsewhere, your hush and ivy fragments along my legs.

There is no breaking what isn't united, you told me, you told me once. Your ditch, your vinyl cove, your timbers. There is no writing that is not looking.

There is an alarm wish economy, and I wish we could buy each other's hours and wrap them up, drench each other in them. You are hard to say because where our bodies dip into each other – it's tonal, pure sound, yesterday and yesterday. Needing you sunlike, like some solar fury, some orbital pull, you determine this or that hour.

You are in bed, above me. I eat my cereal, I eat it and eat. My salaried organs, my tenured love. I have things to say to your elsewhere, like my body is full of blood, it moves at different speeds, and I unfold my morning in what looks like narrative but isn't.

Dismissing the tombless allegory, to ask you to stand for woman, for body, for citizen. The form of disruption, in this case disrupts itself. The process of knowing you, which is knowing me, betrays me.

ENFANCE IV

after Rimbaud

Tonight I'm all lack
I don't know how to be in a body
that wants like this.

Some days I'm saintly good
If I had a balcony I'd pray on it
I'd be so good on it
I'm nasty now but I was once good
I was once historically good
I bled in all the right places,
I covered my tracks.

Once I bled like a sea would
Under a full moon in a coastal shack
It was so animal politics didn't matter
In this fantasy you didn't care
that I was menstruating
and in the morning as you pass the french press
I see my blood between your fingers.

The personal will cease to be political
in utopia. My desire won't be born of lack
but of fullness…
What do you say?

Now I'm studious, look at me, I've only had one drink
I'm sitting here thinking about how I only desire you
because of my fucked up childhood.
You call me because it's rainy, you got off work early,
but I cannot see you tonight, I'm busy
Unbecoming.

The sunset rinses me clean, I'll walk to work tonight
What is it about walking that proves my love for you?
Melancholy legs are sore, tired of holding up
my sounds. Barely an I, I'm all contradiction
There's no way to inhabit this air, this sick polluted air
Your air

Why are you silent?
Why do you care so much about mimesis?
You've abandoned me like a child
Won't you come over! My heart is out to sea
There is no difference between sky and earth
When it's this foggy out.
That's a metaphor for my anguish.
Can you see my head against the window?
I've never believed in the forever of anything
except the wretched present.

Tired of longing,
no one has walked this path
in centuries
and the weeds cut my ankles.
Do you know what I mean about the air?
It's in this state that
I can't remember what birds or rivers are.
Can't change absence to presence
Just like that
I feel like shit

I'm ending this poem now, yes it's over
a hungry ghost,
nothing has changed.

ENFANCE V

Is dying or living more costly
This apartment might as well be a tomb for all I care
I bet the monthly rent's similar to the plot of dirt,
and dirt cleans up just fine.

Even then I'd just pretend to read while I wait for her to call.
I have elbows, they are useless down here.
Now that my only neighbors are worms and shit
I imagine everyone above living in a fog filled hell
They go to art openings in the city, they go back home to their lovers.
You were brave to forget your umbrella.

I can't bear to think of it. Nothing is not night.
Me, I am in my cozy abyss, oh I'm in my lack alright.
All around my body there are things you can't even imagine
You know, like moons and comets falling in love.
But it too is a love you can't possibly believe.

Just try to imagine the way seaweed tells its story to the sea.
See you can't. I don't know why I'm trying to tell you.
The ocean is a myth that always wins.

Down here I know silence well, I am in charge,
I don't have to talk to anyone anymore.
My oars are made of water,
my sapphire is made of steel. Let's go.

Of course I am aware of the sudden chasm, this call
that casts bitter light, that dwells in my attitude.
But now it's your turn. Tell me what unthinkable blaze
you miss me like.

PERMANENT VOLTA

I.

it's time
I thaw for you

your bones
and your right
now

it's time
for love
in the time
of dollar store cutlery

it's time
I let the public sun
in a little

to betray my rising lust
& my moon's transit

where you are
all up in my litter

swiping on the echoes
of my plastic bathtub
and routine clenched jaw

where I grind the language
out of myself

and submerge my painscale
under the lilypads
in your water

my want
un
changed&changing

bent like a sapling

everyone is invited

to my
biggest storm

II.

It's true
I had forgotten
how to be dew

your fractal hands,
etching glacial
syntax

it reroutes me
over there oh
way over there

the over there
objects of

this dry rot
grammar

reroute the demand
demand a rerouting

digestif class
war

when you're this hungry
take it slow

saying Nothing—
you over there:

this shoulder blade
                    soliloquy
          approximated excess
gagged the
                    after all
                    of my want.

lily spectacular, heaving bloom
          and adjustments.

                    I resent
the icy speculum we see by

my margins invoked and
                    dissolved

all hand route and mouth

III.

I like it my way
where I'm hungry
for your synapses
& attention

I write a poem about it
I write all about it
I stand at my window
& I write about it

there are only
shadows
to write about
this early
in the morning

violent—
to be written
and I
resist—

I take apart
my body

to let my being
be a little more

Nothing is not
          borrowed

& hunger
doesn't compromise—

          together we made
               this place

               together
          we can leave it

IV.

I memorize
math's errors
and diamond equations

the stains on your father's shirt
the grammars
of silence

holding the thickness
of my lack

the primal alienations
of my cul-de-sac youth
of my baseball card stats

& like my hormones
heard in trig

everything has an angle
but not everything can be measured

ghost a want

salve of atmosphere

direct, there
      & not—

open mouth like
math and Nothing
cannot be said

say me
say me and say me

with you
I dust off my distance
and descend

this lack is hot

I want more of it

as they say

V.

we wait
our turn to give
each other
keys and faucets

you want to see
my basement

I want to see
your body bent

around my machines

yea we meant to
cruise each other's ghosts

such mock trials

my jargon
in your void

my hunger concept
in your song

bundled
and unmeasurable

my splintered panes
keep me going

                                    here
                        there is a woman
               in me waiting

                                a fantasy
                         of the factory

               fucking on obsolete machines

VI.

I'm insane
for how you dirtied
the dishes

for your economic
scar tissue

a star's membrane
the core of stench

let's get together
and pay some bills today

totally automatic
withdrawal

we love
in a sagging bed
a viable galaxy

our chaos
letters recombined

I ask questions

mysterious &
blatant—

is my boundary
exquisite to you?

is it
knowable?

isn't this
having?

some days I have
to whisper
to be hearable

it's like
if you don't know,
you don't know

& you may know
something else

but if you don't know
you don't know
then you *really* don't know

VII.

there was a time
before time
was strict
and deviant

I capitulated to the
desperate earth
wanting
to rid itself
of causality

all miracle
it rationalized
my dreams

your poem
shows up in my pollution
in my ecological want

your pain
moves my seasons
jagged and strict

I save you
the last slice
of my orange

I know
we will need
to eat more soon

look at how my worlds
want your worlds

look at our worlds
wanting other worlds

porous the mist we
love by

SOVEREIGN EXHAUSTION

SONOGRAM OF AN EARTHQUAKE

to hear the things
we cannot see—
    say
    mutely the ghosts
shuttering cypress trees, provisionally planted
    say
    mutely the permanent footsteps
among the shape of rain
    say
    floating notation of suspense

hear the being seeping out of this easy body
staccato in bright and opal light

suspend me in the edges
of my knowing

★

shook the unlikely field of hay,
    hazy motors
grooming all oblivion

upright pillars
bearing our antiquities
    our local colosseum
    behind us

if you could dare to call that material—
brick upon brick

this is language, underknowing
a hillside

say   spilled ink crescendoing
        in a milky sky

*

say I am listening like geology
the dusting of hay

say that feeling of dust on skin
ringing invisible like the twisted route of breeze

say   I can only feel
a minor rumble or hum or clacking

say   I can only feel
a major air conditioned tractor inventing noise
of rugged rock and distant capital flows
of groomed aprons' stain
        outside the frame

hum this dirge of possibility
        the octaves etched below
        our wheated horizons

say   what's behind the eye's grasp

        the inside of sound

*

mime
this object in my chest

there is no object, they say
no architectonic tone

of semi-public space swelling against
citizenship's crumbling mortar

74

a tectonic shift hurts me
     say burning motor say sparking sound
     say scattered promise of daybreak

overfeeling and saturated
in daylight's golden tones

*

we are sleeping in beds above
grass and all these vibrations

our heads resting heavy on city clouds

leaning into each other's inhale
like voices discovering
the chant etched on an entombed wall

breaking vision
unconcerned with facts

breaking
     desire's glissando

*

each morning
the beautiful

creak or chirp or the mower's social noise

     the total murmur
     of reproductive fact

historical longing, elbows resting on wood

the milky way'd sex
haunting the mirrors

            our mirroring body
            our whole notes
say
the eclipse pace of confronting
            the end of the individual

this is the thing I cannot see
in my portrait

★

to hear the things we cannot see—

say circuit say legacy
say history's glacial rhododendron

            thickened sound disperses us
            in plastered din of the eras
                    that our cupped palms seek to hold

say the wall of a rose, say thorned departure
say humming rain, say sovereign exhaustion

say the billowed vertebrae of all the casual atrocities

say the farmers of the bucolic waste
say we occur despite twisted metal
            rebounding tonal workdays
            flickering our understanding

★

sonogram of the earthquake

in the old town
through the windowsill
I feel the ruined part
        of over there

the caper bush of spring's obscure
blossoms and July's promise of heat

sound waves echo off
the elongated day

      we try seeing with only our chest
a small & delinquent interruption

we could meet each other here
      in those cavities of time

ourselves indistinguishable

*

scatter the pile of thorns
then say
      you   over there
      in each vibrating calcium deposit
the emotional greeting of coda
      I see you in me
      I feel you there

in this clarity this particular love I too feel
the silence of noise contemporary and
diminishing light

say   over there you tone in me
before the beginning made itself
barely heard

BLUR ME OUT

i've been up all night
trying to figure out how to want
loud enough to tie myself up
and out into the after all
of this luxurious thralldom
that keeps me in the way
of myself and my poem's perineal body

autonomous bottom seeking
non-sovereign top
spit up into me
so my digestive track
can get a full night's sleep
while the stars' algorithm
churn out millions
squeezing lightyears, inciting a humming
that clocks my little shapes of pain

they look different erupting
out of this sinkhole of massive unseeing,
my right now controversy vivid and
on lock

i am all submitted to you
like you submit to the blossoming
that happens in the siloed collective gut
and gray water, a bacchanal inside us

we found each other under here
so we return the symbols we bought
we concoct new drives and partial objects
we barricade the speedbumps
disentangle the mission of highways

there where we are mother of each other
where we are brothers
baby birding disobedience
to our sense of self
cashing in on the Real's residue

but here call it stardust, call it umami,
call me nobody, blur me out

POEM IN VERS

*

my arching tower, the flood around my throat
you buzzing angelic, the puddles of your back's silhouette
gauging proximity when it preceded my dream of
your thorny brows, a life before life where
I would be returned to daybreak

my Atlantic missing, my crack of dawn
we stood calmly in our waters, our lovers all
around us & I felt the hard parts of your body
I felt the inside of the feeling and how slow
the sky can move, wrapped in red light

my stigmata'd agave, dizzy my daddy
I look in your room, a box of knots,
chain and breeze, something moved still
& pink. it whispers to me strictly—*look at me,
look at me harder.*

ditch of my wonder, lasso my planets and needs
bind me and bind me, make brother of my stars.

In your objects, not yet knowing
how to know, I still knew how to look

★

your swamps run through my windows and steel
little minnow bubbles like shadows
drawn out of drowning sun
and my coveted shame

be strict my morning glory
be the ringing in my ears
you a cowboy hat for my
obedient neon rose

with raw steak and faded rope
kiss my lava ringtone
        disturb my vined earthworms
        break my babylon

*

here with my poem
in your most occluded
& sticky porn

emphasize my nobody
little ancient voice of mine
and free that way from this life

my paradise, my chiseled pillar
I lay down in your towering
you were taller and taller still

there I saw you clearly
you could split my languages
I could ask you to be God

I knew I couldn't slip
out of your red knots
I saw how you could release
        my tourniquet,
        unearth my need

★

a glimmering dick for your once was
I etched you, reflected on a bible stand
I watched your somnolent rivers

preparing to be
unmade

I'm so far in your bowels
my grace, my taboo boy boy
my thickest saliva, my mistaken little girl
with my mania unshakeable

I demand you
demand me

shake my rotten moonbeams
with your youngest blossom, the sick one,
the no's you couldn't say, each excised
recollection, each culled disappearance

my renowned fool,
my encased hummingbird

it's in us now, the sunset genuflection,
as if to say how rare our chained labyrinth
your weeded shit
your shapes of cloud

*

my cockroached son, saccharine slut, tied-up gas station donkey
the amount of water you drink is my unending desire,
the sky is blue & it bulges, rolling like a newborn,
like our train to Winslow—unutterable

my sacred jimmy, my profane child
on a Gallup highway stretch of double yellow solid lines
raised just centimeters off the steamrolled asphalt
I jam into your ass in a buzzing stall of horse shit

my pink pussy my pink haired love
splashing in your plastic bottles and salted hands
I can have you in grand canyons and motels lime-green curtains
left open for sick palm trees & strip mall tacos to see

big-boned pilot, my all of Arizona
I drank your private property with your mother's
credit card and you name the capitals of the all states
with your sun scorching my vines in my passenger seat

dazzled my faggot, pious my boy of sun
it is perilous to want your milkshakes and shrubs
and Walgreens syringe to make a man of me
in our cul-de-sac ford focus
wanting to make even your fist come

blood born blossom, spit on my face,
ruin my graced language

*

young rat of a school boy, a dewy little prince
swallowing your sweet putrid air of bone

embedded clover shooting forth
in the flux of the rain or sun

I'll be a secretary of your want
with all your rot and black widowed soil

shut me up and let my rage fill your container
melt my most plutonic rock

release my pained solar systems
let me wander our spacious orchards

DITCH SESTINA
for GD

If the answer is yes, keep asking.
Author this submission,
from deep within my affluence.

Devil in reverse.
The sun on our bodies was so warm
I hardly remember my river.

With red ropes disorient my symbols,
my tyrannical metaphors,
make missionary

say love's stolen name:
toothbrush, choked property,
dizzy ghost, ditch of a man.

Nasty baby, blossom your fist,
overflow into my cups.
Be cataclysm. Grow for me G-D.

Cast me as shadow,
and I want to feel each ray.
Give me your whole war.

★

Betray me, you nudist brat, you pathetic inked halo,
you stale rumor of war.

Mythic debris cakes our air. Make me cozy.
Then suffocate my channel of affluence.

Loyal and diurnal, I seethe torrentially in your moonlight.
Kiss my cheek G-D, in your Queen's indebted bed.

Be sickened by my tumult.
Destitute my fungible river.
Burn down my six-winged tears.

Aerated devotion,
scabbed ascension toward man.

Smuggled in your crypts, strolling in your Assisi.
I am each knot, each bursting missionary.

＊

Gush little girl.
Subscribe to my ditch.
Watch me uncarve your river.

You are mulberries in my throat.
You of scratched armor,
a flooded man—
the sweet mud of my boots.

I step in your name,
I dig my spade in your war.

Where you are sun, I train my vines around you.
I name you morning glory.

Poets choke on your rivers,
your rivers choke on me.

Seeping missionary,
Watch me G-D.

A bad man for your water,
a ditch for your fluttering affluence.

*

Settle my ungrateful id,
my trusted missionary.

Lock me in your garden,
organize my earthquake,
turn water into man.

Tie me up to free me,
and never say my name,
fill up my fear of war.

Incite my fear of nothingness,
deluded vowels, discarded affluence.

Fuck me and forget me
Let our thickest milk
grow spoiled

SERENITY POST

day, body, breathing
if i follow this seeing
what city summits can i conceive of
& how deep in the dirt can i
rest my question, unwind my tide
break the law till it's broken
and, together, fossilize
the known measures
hushed like nostalgic traces
of rope marks imprinted
around your wrists.

machine song, my forensic shame
this unconditional love in escrow
where a partial third party mediates my view
of glistening dirt and faded starlight.
i'm scared of the overexposed times
when i disappear you behind yourself
& with sunspotted vision
i'm left with only myself to love.

adoration, reinvented time
some days i whisper my name, quietly, to myself.
a rotund hypocorism, blossom'd and swooping
to usher in a new day-and-age
where the horizon's my trade &
i turn back toward earth,
tilting forward my graced pelvis—
my arched foot, bent around a lucite sun.

ecstatic form, risk, surge
some days i cross titrate myself with clouds
& tidal chores: the earwigs scatter in dismay,
the dust relocates, displacing

the invasive bougainvillea.
little reminders, like thunder, cake the oat encrusted pan—
& i intertwine my aloneness with your piles
of clothy barricade.

kill fuck marry:
the screen/ the window/ the sky
discarding all threshold, possessed
out of possession, i adjust my sense
of what is coming, to what is already here—
       together, the beach crowd calculates distant showers
       a superstitious couple blames the traffic
       mattresses pile up on curbs, creaking
       a detoxed pomegranate branch bends under its blossoms
       spectacular & paranoid, the perennial flowers mask up,
       multiplying like plastic, floating on camouflaged fences.

SOVEREIGN EXHAUSTION

(after Tale by Arthur Rimbaud)

dildonic my massacre
a neo-gloryhole'd liberal fantasy
chafed, devotional and shadowy
this truth
     this piety
generous my justice, a snapped little twig
oozing like dry ice, the other side of desire

embellished the oxytocin that could ever
honeycomb an inbox toward revolution
in total coming together
in synchronic transmission
of global and mountainous deprogrammed love

/

with my poetic prosthesis in your most laced crevasse
i slash the throats of my parking spaces
     my metric days
     my meter fees

i'm always so on time for you
i walk around the block
with the smashed plastic sea shore flooding
past the rocks to the downtown of my heart
just so i'm not too early
and you know my minds tied up
in imagining the casual riot
where the fence isn't chained to fence
     isn't keeping out our staged stamina
keeping track of our charging cycles

/

i am dissolving in the waiting room
of the toyota dealership
an oil change splashed on my pronoun
possessive adjective on corporate forms
waiting out the twisted suspense
of a law firm bailing out
the logic of bail

better to destroy the boat, my aching trees,
than patch the sinking hole

let's start *over*
my ride
my tectonic edgeplay
with the concept of *who i am* showered in
petroleum veins like
i want to be together
but I also want to be left alone
my INFP commie conundrum
my introvert version of togethering
my close to death daisy, my weeded bouquet

/
lilac'd evening approaches
my gilded horror so unspoken
i can finally speak

look now
the evaporation of trauma'd bank accounts
where we annihilate ourselves
to mediate our dyings

this shadow self locked up in self love groupons
this medicaid appointment
a saccharine elixir of redaction—

together in cinderblock'd health
we lack the form to want each other rightly
so my wonder spreads egoic and planless
not wanting to pass as reform
in bonfired bunks & bedridden poems
i ask again, more quietly
rejuvenate my cruelty
for *there is no sovereign music for our desire*

CAESURA FOUNTAIN

my ability to   conjugate is rocky
swapping melted water for genetic grain
cracking sweet stains & seeping wild
winged condensation   into my cluttered
speaking patterns   all caesura'd out

my inch wants   a mile   it wants to
balloon that gap all O's in there
machining a nothingness to
loop and loop under the fountain's infrastructure

where of course   i crave
the imperceptible   stone

i used to speak a language that
shone in   the galvanized pipe-
dream of me, a subsidized starlet
my breath indiscreetly   unknown

i loved and loved that crusted neglect
that secret punishment   so sweet where
water fell   so water   so dusty
with all that caked up future conditional
recycled and trapped in the same   water
as last year   the year before

my machine yearns   for flood and for
fire that can't be put out   with piss
imagination some great stalwart
of discipline   like a strict fungal network
on molly   in the timespace of the marble pores
of being here   holding your hand

a sadness   is stalking me
it's the shape of a chorus   its glitchy
double vision   gone when you look at it
the darkside of the gushing's
shadow   it's down the drain
it's briny cornucopia of   feeling

a total entanglement seeps out of me
i'm drinking gallons of it
i am chugging it   i am hydrated
strange and pissing   all the time

this body   a fountain   of filtered rocket
fuel and helping verbs   unlocatable

i let my caesura grow long as
that old fork   in the road
where the   wood pile rots
when fire   loses interest

his mother always told him
the squeaky wheel   gets the oil
as if oil   hadn't already ended the world

i say   let the wheel squeak
let us squeak until
oil is obsolete   let it rust
while we uninvent   the wheel
let us fall in the wheel's caesura

let the fountain   seep over stone
till we feel the damp tips of our shoelaces
puddled & enmeshed   a marsh to touch
on every surface   the light can't find

pause spewing pause
to learn the grammatical fact—
there is no going   forward alone

Sources

Many texts influenced my thinking and writing across the span of time that I drafted
Permanent Volta. References, allusions, translations, and phrases from the texts below appear
throughout these poems.

Acker, Kathy. *In Memoriam To Identity*. Boyer, Anne. *Garments Against Women*. Brooks,
Gwendolyn. *Riot*. Butler, Judith. *The Psychic Life of Power: Theories in Subjection*. Césaire,
Aimé. *Notebook of a Return to the Native Land*. Clandestine Whores Network. "Sex Workers
Against Work." Dickinson, Emily. *The Poems of Emily Dickinson*. H.D. "Calliope." *Collected
Poems 1912-1944*. Halpern, Rob. *Music for Porn*. Hartman, Saidiya. *Scenes of Subjection:
Terror, Slavery, and Self-Making in Nineteenth-Century America*. Kapil, Bhanu. *Ban en Banlieue*.
Luxemburg, Rosa. *The Letters of Rosa Luxemburg*. Marx, Karl. "Human Requirements and
Division of Labour Under the Rule of Private Property." Moten, Fred *In the Break: The
Aesthetics of the Black Radical Tradition*. Oppen, George. "Of Being Numerous." Rimbaud,
Arthur. Trans. Schmidt, Paul. *Arthur Rimbaud: Complete Works*.

Acknowledgments

To Patricia, the original muse on strike / the always striking muse. You are the actual rock in my pocket. This book is for you, and all the No's. Dina, I drink from your cups every day. Thank you for keeping us all grounded on earth.

Thank you to my friends & comrades: Anna, for being the first to ask what autonomy meant to me. Meg, for your feverdream posters, love poems, and insurrectionary visions. Norah, for teaching me all your tricks. Kristin, for being cloud, for braids full of razor blades, tears to sell; for living as general strike, intricately and exquisitely attuned to care for everything you encounter. Addy, you can really write a poem. To Katie and Bishop, our happy Garland family. Megan, Leander, Bobby, The Vitas, Matt, Allie, Shawntai, Leah. Joe and Sarah, my canal guardian angels. anise, for unorganizing this book into the metaphysical bricks it wants to be. Mel, the original dyke poet. V, Rose, Bella, Wendy. Sacha, you and your void. Hazel, Willa, Asia, Melissa, Julia. To Scripps Street. To Maia, thank you for ushering so much poetry into the world, for showing me you can solve some things in life by moving to LA.

Shayna, for holding it down at Eastern Michigan University and helping us all get paid.

Karmyn, Sara, Colleen, Tracy, Mikayla, and Jennifer, whose poems and conversation have radically nourished my thinking and writing over the past many years.

To my teachers and mentors: Carla, whose invaluable perspective guided me throughout this project. Rob, whose home and library housed me in the year of absence. Thank you for your mentorship, friendship, and our ongoing dialogue.

To the editors who previously published work that appears in this book: *Museums Press / A Plume Annual, MASK Magazine, Jubilat, WONDER, New Delta Review, Apogee, VOLT, Social Text Journal, House Party @ the Poetry Project,* and *Homointern.*

Thank you especially to my generous editors Stephen Motika and Lindsey Boldt at Nightboat Books, and the Nightboat Team, Caelan Nardone, Gia Gonzales, and Lina Bergamini, for all the labor and care that went into this book. Thank you to Brian Teare for choosing *Permanent Volta* for the Sawtooth Poetry Prize and to Janet Holmes for her early support of this work. After Ahsahta's closing, I am deeply grateful to Brian's generosity and dedication in helping it find a home.

It is with awe and gratitude I thank Rissa for envisioning this cover concept: an inversion of Lacan's Graph of Desire, flipping the vector of the split subject on its head and dressing it up in neon vines. The illustration that appears on the cover is the result of Mountain's stunning response to this prompt — thank you for entering this daydream and creating such a beautiful veil.

Thank you, lastly, to my family and their consistent support that suspends common sense. To Elizabeth, for your jokes and your love that levitates me into daily rebirth. Finally & deeply, to Cy, for your ditches and your presence. The rest is all in here.

In addition, this book has been made possible, in part, by grants from the New York City Department of Cultural Affairs in partnership with the City Council and the New York State Council on the Arts Literature Program.